Woven Souls

Love, Longing, Release, and Roots—
reflections woven in verse.

Diyaa N Punjabi

BookLeaf Publishing

India | USA | UK

Made with ❤ on the BookLeaf Publishing Platform
www.bookleafpub.in
www.bookleafpub.com

Dedication

To God—my anchor and divine guide through every step of this journey. This book is a reflection of the grace with which You held my hand and led my heart.

To to my family, whose love, strength, and encouragement have always been my foundation. Each one of you has shaped me into who I am today, and for that, I am eternally grateful.

And my love, whose unwavering

*support and endless patience
have been my greatest
inspiration. Your presence is the
rhythm in my heart, and your
love is the spark that fuels my
words.*

*This book holds my heart, my
haven, my always.*

Preface

"Woven Souls" is a journey through the tender threads of love, the secure knot of family, the quiet ache of longing, and the bittersweet release of letting go. In these poems, each word is a reflection of the heart's deepest desires and the soul's silent surrender. The beauty of love often lies not just in its moments of closeness, but in the space that remains when we must part, when we must let go, and when we must trust that the connections we share never truly unravel.

Some of these poems were written years ago, carefully crafted as I sought to capture the raw, unfiltered emotions that have shaped my experiences. Writing my feelings and thoughts has always been my passion, a way to make sense of the world around me and within me. These words are more than just poems—they are pieces of my heart, woven together over time to create something that I hope resonates with others who have loved, longed, and let go.

"Woven Souls" is an invitation to embrace the complexity of these emotions, to honour the people and moments that shape us, and to find peace in the threads that remain.

Acknowledgements

As I pen this collection, I am deeply grateful to the many souls who have influenced and shaped these words, even in the quietest of moments. To the ones who have loved me, and to those who have left, your presence in my life has been the canvas upon which these poems were born. Each heartache, each whisper of hope, and each tender memory is a reflection of what you brought into my world.

To my family and friends, who have always supported me in my pursuit of writing, your encouragement has been the gentle wind beneath my wings. You have held space for me to explore my emotions, and for that, I am endlessly thankful.

To my readers, past, present, and future, your connection to these words is what gives them life. I hope that in these poems, you find echoes of your own experiences, your own love, your own letting go.

Finally, to the art of writing itself—thank you for being my constant companion, my sanctuary, and my way of understanding the world. Through the act of pouring my heart into these pages, I have found clarity, healing, and a deeper understanding of myself.

This book is for every soul who has ever loved, longed,

or let go. You are woven into these pages, and for that, I am eternally grateful.

1. She Loves, She Shines

*She loves to love, with arms flung
wide,*
A tender flame she cannot hide.
She feels the pulse of every soul,
*An empath born to make them
whole.*
*Her heart's a home, her laugh —
a song,*
*With her, you feel where you
belong.*

She's quick with wit, a spark, a
grin,
A storyteller steeped in skin.
With every glance, a secret
shared,
She's talent wrapped in humor
bared.
She dances light where others
pause,
And gives her all without a
cause.

She shows up bold, she gives her
best,
A healer's hands, a loyal guest.

*She'll build you up, she'll fight
your fight,
She'll stay beside you through
the night.
But sometimes in her selfless
tide,
She lets her own true needs
subside.*

*She craves the air, the sky, the
sea —
A soul unchained, she must be
free.
She'll run through storms just for
the thrill,*

Then crash too hard, against her
will.
She blurs the line, she dives too
deep,
And wakes in messes she can't
keep.

But oh, the joy she brings to all,
She lifts you high, she breaks
your fall.
A firework burst, a fearless
friend,
A wild heart no cage can bend.
She's love and light, a blazing
trail —

A girl whose spirit will never pale

2. The Waxing & Waning of the Moon

The waxing and waning of the
moon
Tells us a tale, soft and true—
A story of quiet, steady growth,
And a shadowed side of pain,
too.

The swift tides crashing on the
shore
Whisper secrets with each rise—

A tale of oneness, deep and whole
And of parting, beneath the skies.

Just like the love we came to know,
In chemistry and hearts combined—
Once lit with laughter, full and bright,
Now echoes we can't seem to find.

*Yet the moon does not stop
phasing,
Nor does the sea forsake the
shore—
They don't keep returning from
simple habit,
But because the moon stirs the
ocean's core.*

*And ours is a love story, too,
That time has tried and time has
shown—
Longing to fall in each other's
arms,*

*Waiting for stars to guide us
home.*

And when the universe aligns,
And the cosmos clears the way,
*We'll dig for love down to our
souls,*
And leave all else to fade away.

3. An Everlasting Love

This love we share, it never ends,
You melt my heart again and
again.
You said you'd trade the world
for me,

We've cried, we've fought, but
still we stay,
Love pulls us back, it finds a way.

So hold me close, don't let me go,

*Wrap me in your arms and let it
show.*
In your love, I've found my light,
Be my shelter every night.
*Hold me, baby, through the
storm,*
In your arms, I feel so warm.

Each day our love begins anew,
With every breath, I fall for you.
Just when I think I've felt it all,
You lift me higher, break my fall.

Even when we're far apart,
You're the rhythm in my heart.

It's been so long since I saw you
smile,
I've missed you every single mile.
Let me in, don't make me wait,
This love we share is truly fate.

So hold me close, just one more
time,
Let me feel your heartbeat
rhyme.
Be my knight, my shining star,
No matter where we are—
You are my home, near or far.

4. I Wish (For Us)

*I wish to cuddle with you all
night, my love,
And keep you awake like an
insomniac.
I want us to drink to our glory,
And get high listening to our
favourite track.*

*I wish to roam the streets
carefree,*

*With no eyes watching, just you
and me.
To lie beneath a sky full of stars,
And make love, wild and messy,
tipsy and free.*

*I wish you'd bring me my
cherished snack,
And feed me—just the way you
always do.
I want to sit by candlelight with
you,
And share the secrets no one
ever knew.*

I wish we'd curl up arm in arm,
With our treasured book laid
across the bed.
Let your love be the only
warmth I need—
Not a blanket, just your
heartbeat instead.

I wish this night would never
end,
We'd stay up late and greet the
dawn.
Wrapped in each other's souls so
tight,

A moment eternal, forever
drawn.

You freed me from my silent
cage,
And gently touched my aching
soul.
You're my man—I'm yours
completely.
And with each day, I love you
more.

5. The Soul I Seek

*Where do you wander, and what
fills your days?
I long to know you in infinite
ways.
What stirs your heart, what
makes you stay?
What dreams have danced and
drifted away?*

What shadows live behind your
smile,
The secrets hidden, sealed in
style?
The tales you guard, both dark
and deep—
The ones you whisper in your
sleep.

Do I live in your thoughts like
you live in mine?
Does your heart echo back this
yearning sign?

Do you crave me, the way I do
you—
With a love so fierce, so wild, so
true?

What would I find if I walked in
your skin—
The fires you fight, the truths
within?
To fathom your soul, to know
your flame,
To lose myself and feel no shame.

*My love won't fade with passing
years,
It grows with joy, it thrives
through tears.
Even if fate won't write our
story,
My heart will hold your silent
glory.*

*So let me near, if just to see
The soul that calls so endlessly.
With your name etched upon my
soul,
I'll leave this world feeling whole*

6. Answered Prayer

I'll pray again beneath the night,
A humble wish, but pure and
bright.
They say that prayers hold
power bright,
When whispered from a heart
alight.

I've been blessed with all that I
need,

But your love is the one thing I
plead.
With every glance, with every
smile,
I feel you've been missing from
my life a while.

I don't want half, or part of you,
All of me longs for all of you.
It's been ages now, I've hoped
and prayed,
To call you mine, to never fade.

So here I pray with all my might,

That I may be yours in this life's
light.
I wish to wake beside you, dear,
And sleep in your arms, year
after year.

A shooting star up high I spy,
I close my eyes and make a sigh,
I ask the stars to help us meet,
To sprinkle stardust at our feet.

I must have prayed for you
before,
A love so deep, forevermore.

For every prayer, for every plea,
You're my answered wish, my
destiny.

7. Chosen by Fate

*I remember the first day I caught
your glance,
Standing so poised, with a quiet
elegance,
A fleeting vision, you stood by
the door,
And in that moment, I wanted
you more.*

A deep, unspoken urge began to
rise,
To know you, to look deep in
your eyes,
To touch your soul where words
can't reach,
A feeling so foreign, yet mine to
keep.

In the quiet of my heart, I knew,
A journey was about to unfold,
This wasn't just a love;
Our paths had crossed for a
reason.

Time seemed to pause when your
eyes met mine,
A warm embrace in a simple
glance,
Maybe it was just a moment's
chance,
But in that instant, my purpose
found its way.

You gave me a reason to smile
that day,
And you still do, year after year,

Out of the vast crowd, you chose
me,
How did I get so lucky? I often
wonder.

You have been the answer to my
deepest prayer,
The fulfilment of all my hopes
and desires,
I must have done a million good
deeds,
That is why I got your love in my
share

8. Where else would I go?

*I miss the warmth of your kiss on
my tender lips,
The way your touch sends me
spinning, losing my grip.
All I need is you, right here,
right now —
And yet you ask me why I'm
still holding on somehow?*

*Where did you find the nerve to
doubt my love?*

To question the fire that you're
always part of?
Each time you speak, you tear at
my soul,
If not for your heart, where else
would I go?

I told you before, and I'll tell you
once more:
You are not some habit I'm
trying to outgrow.
I've etched you deep into my sole
for a reason,
Not to abandon you, lose midway
through the season.

So listen close and hear me loud,
my man —
I wanna walk beside you for
thousand miles, hand in hand.
I wanna build a home where
only laughter stays,
Where your love is the only
thing I hold onto every day.

Will you believe me when I say?
Your light has always been my
guide, my way.
One look at you gives me the
feeling of content

To love you stronger, each day, is

my only intent

Don't ask me why I choose to

stay—

I'd need a thousand lives to say.

If still you doubt the love I show,

then, love, I'll open palms... and

let you go.

If you were written in my skies,

no time could blur those fated

ties.

Two strangers met—a spark, a

beat—

not every day do soulmates meet.

9. The Light that guides my Soul

When darkness falls and hope is
thin,
you lift me up, you pull me in.
You breathe the strength into my
soul,
you make the broken pieces
whole.

You are the light that breaks my
night,

a beacon burning pure and
bright.
You guide my steps, you lead the
way,
outshining even the golden day.

You are the joy to which I cling,
the song my heart delights to
sing.
Your laughter wraps me like the
skies,
your love's the fire in my eyes.

We bicker, yes, we sometimes
spar,

but never stray too far from star.
For through each fall, our love
ascends,
and so we find our hearts again.

I pledge my soul, my heart, my
hand,
to walk with you across the
land.
This love is rare, this love is true,
my soul now mirrors all of you.

10. You Promised You'd Stay

You promised me you'd always
be near,
By my side through every month
and year.
But life, it seems, had other
plans—
Now I face the days without
your hands.

A single day without you feels so
long,
Like a silent verse in an
unfinished song.
This emptiness, no words can
fill,
A quiet ache that lingers still.

The distance between us
stretches wide,
And with it, my right to stand by
your side.
To hear your voice as hours drift
by,

To read your "I love you" under

every sky.

This life feels fleeting, slipping

through,

Like sand in glass—I'm racing

too.

I don't want us to be apart,

Not even for a second of the

heart.

I need you now, close and clear,

To feel your presence, to draw

you near.

Not just for you to miss me too,

*But to ease the ache of missing
you.*

*I sit and stare at the quiet wall,
Wishing this longing didn't
weigh at all.
This day feels endless, heavy,
slow—
Because I miss you more than
you know.*

11. What Have I Given You?

What have I given, to stir your
heart so true?
Just the bare soul of me, nothing
grand, nothing new.
No riches, no promises carved in
stone—
Just my love, and yet, you make
it your own.

You say "I love you" like it's the
simplest thing,
Yet it carries the weight of a
thousand springs.
You don't just call me your
queen in jest—
You honour me with care, and
treat me the best.

I long to be your unwavering
light,
Even more than you've been
mine.
Though love isn't weighed or
measured,

*It's a depth I yearn for you to
define.*

*You speak of a bond that
transcends time,*
*Of souls entwined in a vow once
sworn—*
*From lifetimes past to the one
we live now,*
Destined to love, to be reborn.

*Sometimes I wonder, is this love
even real?*
*For I've never felt such warmth
before.*

*Is this fate, mere luck, or divine
will?
Perhaps I am blessed
forevermore.*

*So I'll cast away every doubt and
every fear,
No longer questioning what
feels so dear.
For I want to cherish this love
we share,
Far beyond the stars, beyond all
time.*

12. Love in Lockdown

*Never in my wildest imaginings
Did I ever foresee this —
That being apart from you would
Become a bittersweet ache in
this lockdown.*

*My tear-streaked eyes endlessly
search
For the comfort of your tender
soul,*

My heart still wanders, calling
for you,
A yearning now far beyond my
control.

I long for the dawn's first light,
When I would race just to catch
your smile.
Those fleeting morning drives,
Where for a few precious
moments, I could hold you tight.

I reminisce about the beautiful
twilight,

And you, guiding me through
the roads,
My head nestled upon your
shoulder
After we'd spent a perfect day
together.

My mind adores you more each
day,
More than my soul could ever
say.
This distance keeps your touch
confined,
But not the love you left behind.

*I remember when my day would
never end
Without the sight of your
beloved face.
I would surrender anything to
relive that,
To wander down the lanes of
those cherished memories.*

*Return to me, my love,
If only for a moment, fill the
emptiness in my heart.
I promise, I will make my soul a
haven,
Where you will find peace, joy,
and endless love.*

13. A Love Like Yours

My world was never truly empty

—

It held a thousand reasons to go

on.

I lived in peace, wrapped in

sanity,

Yet missed someone I could lean

upon.

Just when I thought I understood,

And feelings lay buried deep
inside,
You came and touched my soul
so gently—
In your joy, my heart began to
glide.

You opened up a brand-new way,
A path I'd only dreamt was real.
You offered me a world reborn,
Where only purest love I feel.

You're the reason behind this
smile,
The sparkle dancing in my eyes,

The quiet warmth within my
soul,
The light that brightens up my
skies.

I hear your voice, even in silence,
A whisper drifting through the
air.
Each time you say how much
you love me,
My heart feels lighter, free and
fair.

With you, I've found my truest
home,

*Not built of walls, but heart and
grace.
In every look, in every touch,
I find my safest, sweetest place.*

14. Of Love and Life

*Beneath the sky where rose and
amber play,
The ocean sighs in whispered,
lilting rhyme.
Two hearts in step along the
shore's soft clay,
Where seagulls dance and tides
forget the time—
There blooms a love more vast
than words can say.*

*Life stirs within the hush of
forest green,
Where sunlight paints the leaves
in golden lace.
Through storms and stillness, joy
and pain between,
The soul finds strength in every
silent place—
Its worth revealed in all that lies
unseen.*

*The sapphire sea, the blush of
twilight air,
Reflect the hues of love's eternal
flame.*

*It lingers sweet through sorrow
and through care,
A steadfast light no shadow
dares to tame,
A vow unspoken, yet forever
there.*

*So let the winds recite their
ageless song,
Let moonlight fall on waves in
silver thread.
For life is short, but love is ever
strong,
And though the stars may blink
and softly shed,*

*Its flame, like dawn, shall burn
the whole night long.*

15. Echoes of the Heart

In the quiet hours, the ache is
deep,
A longing for love I can no
longer keep.
You slipped through my grasp,
like sand in the breeze,
Leaving behind only memories
that freeze.
In my heart, your absence still
makes me weep.

The echoes of your name linger
like night,
Each whisper of the past holds
on so tight.
I search for you in dreams, but
find no trace,
Only the shadows of your warm
embrace.
Still, your absence burns with
unrelenting light.

Our love now a story of broken
refrain,
A symphony played with notes
of pain.

The laughter we shared is lost in
the dark,
While your ghost still lingers,
leaving a mark.
Yet I long for you, despite the
strain.

Though we're apart, you're
etched into my soul,
A silent ache that I can't control.
The time between us may try to
divide,
But in my heart, you'll forever
reside.

In the quiet, your absence still

takes its toll.

16. Gone too Soon

The bouquet looked so fresh,
As did the roses in full bloom—
Pretty pinks and vibrant reds,
Arranged in elegant hues.

Yet, what went unnoticed
Were the dainty filler greens,
The quiet souls that held it all,
Giving life to the scene.

Still, in the shadow of beauty,
They stood unseen and small,
Lonely among the brilliant
shades,
Feeling they did not belong at all.

Little did they know their worth
—

Without them, all would fade.
Their quiet grace and steady
strength

*Brought every color to life and
stayed.*

*I wish you knew you weren't a
misfit,
That you belonged among us
here.
I saw your struggle to find
yourself,
Wandering lost, consumed by
fear.*

You were the light in our world,

The warmth at every turn.
Your smile could melt the coldest
sorrow,
Your presence made hearts burn.

So what went wrong? I still
wonder—
How did your glow grow dim?
A candle never loses its light
By igniting another's flame
within.

If only I could turn back time,

Restore the spark within your
eyes,
Guide you home before you
slipped
Beyond my reach, beyond the
skies.

I miss you—words now fail me,
Emptied by the weight of loss.
My eyes are dry, my heart is
heavy,
Bearing the cost of what is lost.

I hope you've found your peace
at last,
A haven where your soul can
rest.
Know that I loved you deeply
still,
And in my memory, you live yet.

17. "The Heart of Children"

*In the gentle light of morning's
grace,
Where innocence paints a tender
face,
Children's hearts beat pure and
true,
A world of love in all they do,
Their love, a river flowing
through.*

With hands so soft, with eyes
that gleam,
They hold the stars within their
dream.
Sincerity, like morning dew,
Clings to them, both bright and
new,
A warmth that makes the world
feel new.

Their laughter dances on the air,
A melody beyond compare.
No masks they wear, no hidden
art,

*Just boundless love from every
heart,
A gift of peace that sets us apart.*

*In their small hands, the future
lies,
Like gentle winds, they softly
rise.
They bless the earth with each
small prayer,
A whispered hope that fills the
air,
In every breath, a love so rare.*

Oh, how they teach with eyes so
wide,
The depth of love, uncurled,
untied.
A simple touch, a hug, a smile,
They heal the world, they make
it worthwhile,
With every step, they bridge the
miles.

In children's love, the world is
blessed,
Their purity, the truest test.
For in their hearts, the truth we
see—

*A love that's endless, wild, and
free,*
A blessing given to you and me.

18. Thank you Mom

At first, I thought of gifting you the world's most precious things

—

But then I realised, nothing could ever match what you've given us.
So I wondered: what could I offer you that is meaningful and lasting?

Then it came to me—words.

*Not just any words, but the kind
that live on.
Yet even the richest dictionaries
fell short
When I searched for the right
ones to thank you
For all the little things—
The countless, quiet, powerful
things you've done for me.*

*Thank you—
For guiding me when others
misled,
For believing in me when others
doubted,*

*For appreciating me when
others criticised,
For motivating me when others
discouraged,
For supporting me when others
refused to,
For seeing worth in me when
others couldn't.*

*I don't know what I did to
deserve someone like you,
But I know I'm endlessly
grateful.
Grateful to Him for placing you
in our lives,*

Grateful to you for being there

for us.

19. The One Who sent Me

*Before I opened the eyes of
silliness,
I made a vow with quiet
stillness.
To return within the time I set,
A promise to myself I won't
forget.*

*The day I saw the earth's first
light,*

The world around me felt so
right.
I saw Ma—the most beautiful
sight,
And knew in her arms, life took
flight.

This gift of life I did embrace,
With open arms and steady
pace.
To face the unknown, wild and
wide,
And find the truths the stars
would hide.

As days repeated, sorrow came,
With lessons wrapped in quiet
flame.
No gain exists without some
pain,
So every try would not be vain.

Then love arrived and held my
hand,
And showed me beauty sweet
and grand.
But fleeting was its warming
song,
It left me wiser, brave, and
strong.

A friend appeared, both kind and
true,
Who shared my thoughts and
feelings too.
He told me my life was not
complete,
And echoed courage in each
heartbeat.

Now I know that friend so dear,
Was the one who brought me
here.
The one who shaped both stars
and sea—

The one who breathed this soul

in me.

20. Juat For Wonders

A little hand fixed in mine
Goes with me, everywhere I go
Just for wonders
Who needs a companion
When our best mates are these
little souls

Those ceaseless giggles right
from heart
Play like music to my ears

Just for wonders
Where's the time to whine today
When the joy begins to manifest
in such early years

When I miss out on fables and
stories
I see a small mouth that prompts
Just for wonders
Who needs these fictitious
reminders
When this sweet little guide is
here

*Those timely kisses that touch
my cheek
To tell me how precious I am
Just for wonders
Who even needs a lover to
convey
What this cute affectionate kid
can*

*When the best chords strike my
ear
They come from Most tender
tongue
Just for wonders*

'I love u' never sounded so
heavenly
Even in the bestest songs ever
sung

When those delicate fingers dry
my eyes
At the slightest of dampness in
them
Just for wonders
I wud never need additional ally
to do
What this amicable heart can
understand

This role given to me by Him
Has changed my life for best
Just for wonders
Who even needs showy name n
fame
When being a mother to
someone means just the same!!!

Bound by Cosmic Fate

When the stars blinked and the
flowers bloomed
The oceans danced in love so
deep and true
The mountains cheered up in
high spirits
And the sun whispered sweet
nothing to the moon

The whole of universe moved in
prefect accord
It felt nothing short of a miracle
The winds carried the scent of
love through the air
That's when you and me met out
of nowhere

Who are we even to defy this
love
That the gods themselves have
woven together
It's not everyday that two lovers
collide

*He made our paths cross for a
reason for sure*

*You, my love, are a man of
boundless kindness,
I count my blessings twice when
I think of you
I am grateful—to the gods and to
you—
For granting me the grace to
witness a love so true*

*Ours is a love destined to endure
forever;*

And In my heart and soul, I
belong to you.
This is a marriage of two eternal
spirits,
A sacred bond I will always
cherish

I know your love for me runs
deeper than life itself,
And that you would lay down
your breath for me
But that is not what I would ever
wish for,
For without you, my love, what
would life even be?

22. To the Queen with Velvet Paws

*She moves like dusk in softened
grace,
a hush of brown, a swirl of grey,
with eyes that hold the kind of
gaze
that turns the busiest heart to
stay.*

*Her fur, a quilt of twilight shades,
spills like silk across the floor,*

and when she blinks—it's slow,
serene—
as if she's seen the world before.

She's not just cat, she's family
thread,
a silent voice, a gentle bond.
Her purrs are prayers in quiet
rooms,
her presence something we lean
on.

She curls where love feels most
alive,
on folded clothes or laps at rest—

reminding us, in simple ways,
that home is where she lays her
chest.

So here's to her, our velvet
queen,
whose grace we'll never take for
granted.
In a world so loud, so rushed, so
wide—
she's the stillness we never knew
we wanted.

23. The City and the Quiet I Dream

The city breathes in static tones,
its pulse a blur of glass and steel.
Crowds pass like currents, eyes
downcast,
each life a secret it won't reveal.
So much is said, but nothing is
heard—
even laughter feels rehearsed.

The towers rise like silent guards,

but offer no embrace, no face.
The night glows bright with
sleepless light,
but stars have long since left this
place.
Here, the hours race, but never
land,
and kindness feels out of place,
unplanned.

Yet deep within this restless
sprawl,
I dream a door that opens wide—
a home where names are never
lost,

where time moves slow, and
hearts reside.
A table set not just with food,
but stories, hands, and gratitude.

I want to build a gentler space,
where silence heals, not weighs
you down.
Where children grow with dirt-
stained joy,
and no one wears a plastic
crown.
A porch, a garden, wind that
sings—

not wealth, but peace, in simple
things.

So let the city chase its light—
I'll plant a lantern in the dark.
A place where souls remember
soul,
where warmth returns to every
spark.
Not perfect—no—but true and
near,
a place of love, and touch, and
clear.

24. In This Quiet Love

*We didn't choose each other
in the way stories often begin—
no sparks drawn from fairy tales,
just a quiet crossing
meant to be written in time.*

*And though we've had our
moments—
those little storms we weather,*

the words that sometimes miss
their mark—
you are still my calm,
my steady,
my best friend in the noise.

You understand me
not because I'm always clear,
but because you listen
to the parts of me I don't know
how to say.
That kind of love
isn't loud—
it just stays.

No need for perfect promises.
What we have is deeper—
a thread that runs through our
days,
woven through dishes and
laughter,
through tired eyes and shared
dreams,
through little hands that call us
Mom and Dad.

Let's hold this marriage
like something we tend to,

*not something we expect to
bloom on its own.
Let's choose kindness in the
pauses,
grace when it's hardest,
and respect even when we feel
far.*

*Our children will see—
not just love,
but effort,
tenderness,
and the way two people
keep learning to love each other
over and over again.*

We may not have made grand
vows,
but what we live
every day
is promise enough.

And I would choose this life
with you
in every version of the story
we could have told.

25. To My Sons, For the Roads Ahead

*When the world opens wide like
a storm or a sky,
and your questions outnumber
the stars up high,
I won't give you maps, just truth
to recall—*

you were not born to be perfect,
but to stand tall.

Be the man who listens before he
replies,
who doesn't need fists to show
he is wise.
Strength isn't noise—it's in
holding your ground
when the world pulls you low
but your soul won't stay down.

Respect every woman—not just
the ones

you love or admire when the
morning sun runs.
See her not as a mirror of worth
or a prize,
but a full universe with her own
fire and skies.

Don't fear your dreams, even
when they seem steep.
Climb with scraped hands, run
while you weep.
The path may not shimmer, the
crowd may not cheer,
but keep going forward—your
purpose is near.

*Let no one shame you for the
tears that you cry.
They're the proof you're alive—
not weak, but why
you'll love more deeply, lead
with care,
and find joy in places most men
wouldn't dare.*

*Laugh loudly. Fall often. Make
peace with the mess.
Fun is not failure, it's part of
success.*

*Dance like a fool, kiss under the
rain,
and never trade wonder for
fortune or fame.*

*Life's not a race, it's a rhythm, a
song.
It won't always be fair, and it
won't feel long.
So find something sacred, and
give it your all—
a craft, a cause, a voice to call.*

*And when you feel lost—as
someday you will—
come back to the quiet, come
back to the still.
There's wisdom in silence, in
breath, in delay,
and love that will find you, come
what may.*

*Be brave, be kind, be wild, be
true.
And know there is nothing more
proud than you.
Not for what you will own, or
how far you will roam,*

but for living with honor—and

always coming home.

26. When Silence Spoke the Divine

In the hush where silence lays,
not absence—but a thousand
plays:
a pause in speech, a sacred bell,
a scream the soul has learned to
quell.

It hums in ink, it sings in space,
a lover's breath just out of place
—

not nothingness, but something spun

from all the things we leave undone.

Then came the ecstasy—not lust,
but rapture wrapped in mortal dust.
A climax of the heart and mind,
a touch that leaves all time behind.

It wasn't just the body's fire,

but awe that stung and pulled me
higher.
A painting's gasp, a whispered
name—
the sacred ache that knows no
shame.

And then—the divine. No form,
no face,
no priest or proof, no saving
grace.
It bloomed within the breaking
skin,
a presence found not out—but in.

A taste in bread, a child's stare,

the void that buzzes full with

prayer.

Not just a god, but what is true

when silence, ecstasy, and you

become

the same unspoken hue.

27. In Threefold Thread

In the quiet hum of morning
light,
Love *stirs softly, bold yet bright.*
It's the warmth of a hand held
near,
A whispered word that calms
our fear.
Life *is the dance, the twists, the*
turns,

A road we walk where each
heart learns.
Through laughter, tears, and
dreams we chase,
Finding meaning in time's
embrace.
Friendship's the anchor, steady
and true,
A bond that binds in every hue.
It's the laughter shared, the
silent glance,
A rhythm found in life's true
dance.
Together they weave, love, life,
and friends,

An endless story that never
ends.
Through every high, through
every low,
They teach us how to live and
grow.

28. Awaken the Warrior

*You were never meant to shrink
to fit,
You were born of stars—every
spark, legit.
The storm you fear was sent to
teach,
That power lives within your
reach.*

Let gratitude not be soft and
small,
But fierce—like flames that never
fall.
Say thank you to the cracks, the
breaks,
They're the ground from which
your purpose wakes.

Compassion is not weakness, no
—

It's strength that lets the true
self show.
To hold another's pain as light,
Is to wage love's war and win
the fight.

Stand tall in truth, don't blur the
line,
Self-awareness is not a sign
Of doubt—but knowing where
you bend,
So you can rise, not just pretend.

Be grateful not for ease alone,
But for the seeds that pain has
sown.
The morning breeze, a glance, a
sigh—
Are miracles the blind pass by.
To count the small is to ignite

A soul that sees with sacred

sight.

Now go, rewrite the story told.

You are not broken—you are

bold.

Live like your breath ignites the

air—

With strength, with soul, with

wild care.

29. "Here and Enough"

Don't wait by doors that never
knock,
Or count the hours on a silent
clock.
Life whispers now, not some far
when—
The treasure lies in where you've
been.

Your worth is not a borrowed
flame,

Not stitched to someone else's
name.
You are the sun that learns to
rise
Even when clouds veil the skies.

Seek meaning in the morning
breeze,
In laughter shared, in rustling
trees.
In hands you hold, in steps you
take,
In love you give, not just what
breaks.

*If fate decides, they'll walk your
way,
A soul aligned, come what may.
But if they pass, don't dim your
light—
Not all that leaves was never
right.*

*Some stays are short, but sweet
and wide,
Like waves that kiss, then leave
the tide.
Be grateful for the moments
passed,
Not everything is meant to last.*

So dance today, unchained, alive,
You don't need someone to
arrive.
You are the meaning you pursue
—
And life is rich because of you.

30. Held by Light

Each morning,
You greet me with wonder—
sunlight spilling across my skin,
a breeze that knows my name.
You are there
before my eyes even open,
reminding me:
I am never alone.
You build my faith
not in thunder,

but in the quiet certainty
that I am loved—
in the way flowers bloom
without needing permission,
and the stars show up
even when no one is watching.
You guide me gently—
a whisper in the noise,
a nudge when I wander,
a hand that holds mine
even when I forget
to reach back.
Miracles?
Yes—
I see them now.
In laughter shared,

in time slowed down,
in words that arrive
when I need them most.
In the timing that feels divine
because it is.
You stayed with me
when skies turned grey,
when the path disappeared.
But even then—
You lit new ways
under my feet.
You made me brave
without asking me to be.
And now,
each day is touched with Your
light.

Each moment,
an invitation to trust.
Each breath,
a reminder that love is real,
and You—
You are always here.
My strength,
my guide,
my grace.
My only Constant.
My forever Yes.